Animals are the Funniest People

by Professor Percy Niwrad

ARGUS COMMUNICATIONS
Niles, Illinois

FIRST EDITION

© Copyright Argus Communications 1976.

Printed in the United States of America.

ARGUS COMMUNICATIONS
7440 Natchez Avenue
Niles, Illinois 60648

International Standard Book Number: 0-913592-75-7
Library of Congress Number: 76-20246

3 4 5 6 7 8 9 0

Photo Credits

Cover: K. W. Fink/BRUCE COLEMAN

Chapter 1 Office
Robert McKendrick 5
D. & R. Sullivan/BRUCE COLEMAN 6
Grant Heilman 7
Lynn M. Stone 8
Grant Heilman 9
Jen & Des Bartlett/BRUCE COLEMAN 10
D. & R. Sullivan/BRUCE COLEMAN 11
Grant Heilman 12
Jack Couffer/BRUCE COLEMAN 13
Jen & Des Bartlett/BRUCE COLEMAN 14
G. Harrison/BRUCE COLEMAN 15
Barbara Adams/FPG 16
Joe Van Wormer/BRUCE COLEMAN 17
Theodore F. Welch/VAN CLEVE 18

Chapter 2 Career
Brent Jones 21
Lynn M. Stone 22
Norman Owen Tomalin/BRUCE COLEMAN 23
F. Erize/BRUCE COLEMAN 24
Norman Owen Tomalin/BRUCE COLEMAN 25 (top)
Laura Riley/BRUCE COLEMAN 25 (bottom)
J.H. Carmichael, Jr./BRUCE COLEMAN 26
O.S.F./BRUCE COLEMAN 27
Norman Owen Tomalin/BRUCE COLEMAN 28
Jane Burton/BRUCE COLEMAN 29
John Running/STOCK BOSTON 30
M.P.L. Fogden/BRUCE COLEMAN 31
D. & R. Sullivan/BRUCE COLEMAN 32
H. Reinhard/BRUCE COLEMAN 33
Audrey Ross/VAN CLEVE 34
Leonard Lee Rue/VAN CLEVE 35
Jeff March 36
G. Harrison/BRUCE COLEMAN 37
N. Devore III/BRUCE COLEMAN 38
Ed Simonek 39
Grant Heilman 40
A.J. Hewerdine/BRUCE COLEMAN 41
Bruce W. Coleman/BRUCE COLEMAN 42
H. Albrecht/BRUCE COLEMAN 43
Robert McKendrick 44

Chapter 3 Types
Jerry Lesser/BRUCE COLEMAN 47
Jane Burton/BRUCE COLEMAN 48
Alan Blank/BRUCE COLEMAN 49
Daniel Stouffer, Jr. 50
Jack Couffer/BRUCE COLEMAN 51
Alan Foley/ALPHA 52
G. Harrison/BRUCE COLEMAN 53
H. Albrecht/BRUCE COLEMAN 54
Robert Frerch 55
Charles Luchsinger 56 (top)
Harry Engels/BRUCE COLEMAN 56 (bottom)
Audrey Ross/BRUCE COLEMAN 57
Jim Ferri 58
K.W. Fink/BRUCE COLEMAN 59
Zimmerman/FPG 60
D. & R. Sullivan/BRUCE COLEMAN 61

Chapter 4 Politicians
Ed Cooper 63
P. Ward/BRUCE COLEMAN 64
Carolyn Wood/VAN CLEVE 65
L. Riley/BRUCE COLEMAN 66
G. B. Schaller/BRUCE COLEMAN 67
Bruce W. Coleman/BRUCE COLEMAN 68
Grant Heilman 69
Grant Heilman 70 (top)
Joe Van Wormer/BRUCE COLEMAN 70 (bottom)
Audrey Ross/VAN CLEVE 71
Jane Burton/BRUCE COLEMAN 72
Norman Myers/BRUCE COLEMAN 73
Thase Daniel/BRUCE COLEMAN 74
Norman Owen Tomalin/BRUCE COLEMAN 75
John S. Flannery/BRUCE COLEMAN 76
Mark Rosenthal/VAN CLEVE 77
Tom Stack/TOM STACK & ASSOC. 78
Lynn M. Stone 79
Norman Owen Tomalin/BRUCE COLEMAN 80
Robert McKendrick 81

Chapter 5 Church
Joe Van Wormer/BRUCE COLEMAN 83
Simon Trevor/BRUCE COLEMAN 84
J.M. Burnley/BRUCE COLEMAN 85
Jessica Ehlers/BRUCE COLEMAN 86
I. Polunin/BRUCE COLEMAN 87
M.P. Kahl/BRUCE COLEMAN 88
J.M. Bishop/BRUCE COLEMAN 89
Robert McKendrick 90
Leonard Lee Rue/ALPHA 91
Robert McKendrick 92
Brent Jones 93
Lynn M. Stone 94 (left)
Robert McKendrick 94 (right)
Lynn M. Stone 95

Chapter 6 University
Norman Owen Tomalin/BRUCE COLEMAN 97
Bruce W. Coleman/BRUCE COLEMAN 98
Allan Bruce Zee/VAN CLEVE 99
VAN CLEVE 100
H. Reinhard/BRUCE COLEMAN 101
K.W. Fink/BRUCE COLEMAN 102
Jane Burton/BRUCE COLEMAN 103 (left)
Jack Couffer/BRUCE COLEMAN 103 (right)
G. Zahm/BRUCE COLEMAN 104
Herta Newton 105
Dana Brown/FPG 106
G. Harrison/BRUCE COLEMAN 107
Steve Hurwitz/BRUCE COLEMAN 108
Peter Fronk/VAN CLEVE 109
G.D. Dodge & D.R. Thompson/BRUCE COLEMAN 110
Albert Bendelius/VAN CLEVE 111

Chapter 7 Epilogue
Ben McCall/FPG 113
George Mars Cassidy/VAN CLEVE 114
Grant Heilman 115
J. Markham/BRUCE COLEMAN 116
A. Ross/BRUCE COLEMAN 117
Laura Riley/BRUCE COLEMAN 118
Barbara Adams/FPG 119
Jen & Des Bartlett/BRUCE COLEMAN 120

Introduction

The study of animal expression has been a revelation.
Instead of scientific data, I keep discovering creatures
that look like my wife's relatives and other assorted
friends. Having made this statement, I, of course,
apologize to my creatures.

You might have doubts about the value of my work.
But wait! As you go through this book
you will see many people you know. You will see
the expression of many feelings you have experienced.
Please don't laugh at my creatures.
Remember, every one of them has a mother, too.

CONTENTS

CHAPTER 1

Unreal as it seems,
One of the unexpected plusses
of my research is that
I have been able to
completely staff an office
with my creatures.

Some say that an office
Is like a zoo,
Why do you think
They hold this view?

Chairman
of the
Board

President and Vice-President

Treasurer

Production Manager

Quality Control Director

Controller

Receptionist

**Advertising
Manager**

The
Boss's
Son

**Principal
Stockholder**

14

Salesman

**Time
and
Motion
Analyst**

Planning Committee

Supervisor and Workers

CHAPTER 2

Most animals don't work
and don't need to work.
But I'm sure you will
agree my creatures
possess characteristics
undeniably associable
with certain careers.

Humans work and worry
and wait to retire and play.
Animals just rove and romp—
All their time is spent that way.

Lifeguard

Throat Doctor

Theatre
Critic

Bankers

Friendly Loan Company Representative

Loan Applicant

Encyclopedia
Salesman

Private Eye

Linebacker

Sports
Announcer

Used Car Salesman

Traveling Salesman

Coach

Basketball Player

Psychiatrist and Patient

Teacher

Astronaut

Hit Man

Insurance Salesman with Client

Plumbers

Entrepreneur

Quiz
Show
MC

Hairdresser

Masseuse

Interior Decorator

CHAPTER 3

"You know the type,"
often succinctly expresses
a whole world of information.
Although animals abhor stereotyping,
I could not resist
sharing my discovery with you.

Typing my creatures
Is really not fair,
But if you see what I see,
The facts are all there.

I told you so!

**Monday
Night
Football
Announcers**

Who, me?

I was sure we parked in aisle 4.

Oh, do you really think I've lost weight?

Quit asking how much further it is.

It's not
too bad
for a
California
wine.

Things never
seem as bad
as they are

**Professor Percy Niwrad
shortly after
his research was
completed.**

I love contact sports.

I think I'd better
wait until tomorrow.

What do
you mean,
everybody
out!

It was
nothing,
really.

Yes, well
I've got this
terrible
hay fever.

Wow,
is she
built!

I know
I promised
not to talk
politics, but...

CHAPTER 4

Politicians

Politicians are people, too,
with peculiarities of
both habit and habitat.
The candidate is no
less idiosyncratic than
you or me, but he does
come in special varieties.

The politician, bless his soul,
Will show an innate flair:
He'll be mugging and shrieking
While whaling his arms in the air.

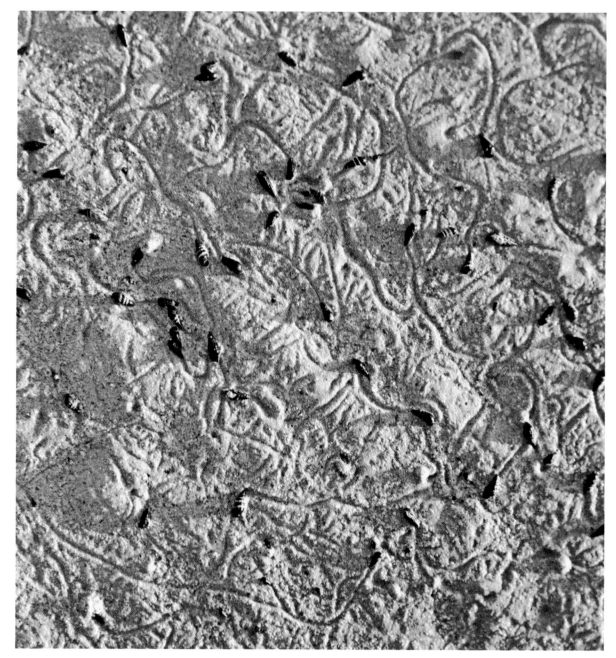

Congressional
Planning
Committee

I refuse
to testify
on the grounds
that it may
incriminate me.

Minority and Majority Leaders

The Vocal Minority

The Silent Majority

The Senior Senator from the great state of...

**Supreme
Court
Justice**

Republican Caucus

**Democrat going to
a fund-raising banquet.**

Press Secretary

I have
the great
honor to
nominate...

A vote
for me
is a vote
for absolute
equality!

Commisars Discussing Crop Failure

Unsuccessful Russian Farmer

Chinese Delegation to the United Nations

American Isolationist

**Internal Revenue
Service Agent**

Taxpayer

CHAPTER 5

I was astounded to see
resemblances continue through the
men of the cloth. Dare I
publish these dramatic findings—
that religious are human too?
With Galilean gallantry
I dared.

If these were the days
Of the Spanish Inquisition,
I would have shown
Much more inhibition.

TM Guru

The Saint

The
Reformer

The
Choir Leader

The
Theologian

Group Baptism

The Heretics

The Ecumenists

The Fundamentalist

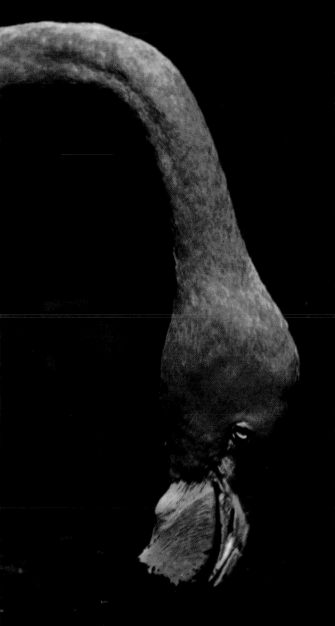

The Charismatic

The Penitent

The Prophet

CHAPTER 6

Academia seems so proper,
ordered and informed.
Is it possible that
my very colleagues could
appear in this bizarre
marriage of species?
It was unavoidable.

It is here I base my case
For some specie to specie associations—
Even amongst the hallowed halls
We discover new animal relations.

How can
I pick
the right
university?

Incoming Freshman

Incoming Freshman's Roommate

**Chairman of
Psychology
Department**

Futurist

Researcher

Botanist

103

Law Students

University
President

Speech Instructor

**The Morning
After the Party**

Philosophy Professor

**Tenured
Professor**

Academic Procession

ALMOST FAMOUS PEOPLE

Of all sad words
Of tongue or pen,
The saddest are these:
"It might have been."
JOHN GREENLEAF WHITTIER

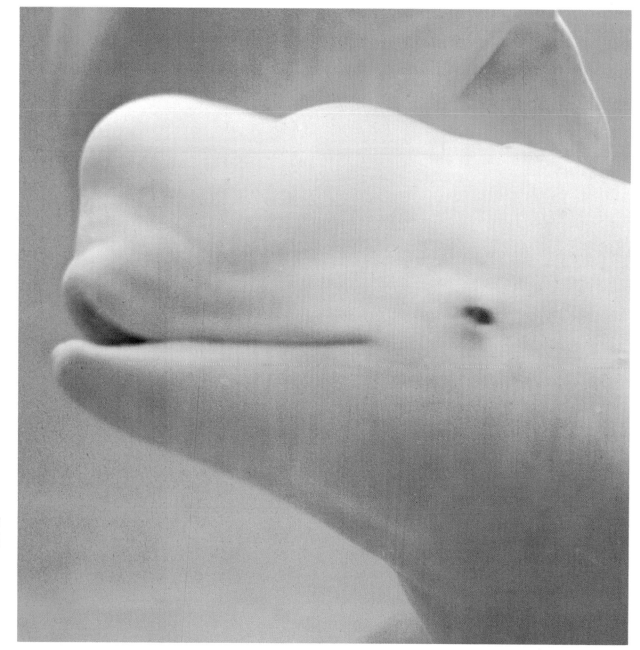

**Moby
Richard**

**The Second Chicken
to Cross the Road**

Abby Landers

Romeo and Gertrude

Sears and Blowbuck

Jean Houndlow

Bella La Ghostie